in the stillness meditations to read
by Jim Ryan

in the stillness *by* Jim Ryan

Published by Eternity Ink

Email: bkmedia@ozemail.com.au

©2000 Brahma Kumaris Raja Yoga Centres Australia Inc.

ISBN 0 9587230 2 8

This book has been produced by the Brahma Kumaris World Spiritual University, a non-profit organisation, with the aim of sharing spiritual knowledge as a community service for the personal growth of individuals. The Brahma Kumaris World Spiritual University exists to serve the family of humanity: to assist individuals to discover and experience their own spirituality and personal growth; to understand the significance and consequences of individual actions and global interactions; and to reconnect and strengthen the eternal relationship with the Supreme Soul, the spiritual parent.

contents

In the Stillness offers an oasis of tranquil and refreshing thoughts. The meditations guide the mind away from the turbulence of spinning thoughts into the calm, still waters of the soul's purity, helping to ease worries, fears and accumulated

INTRODUCTION

hurts. The messages guide the journey inwards to a personal world where you can begin to understand and reconcile many feelings and emotions. Using this still, peaceful state of mind, you tap inner wisdom, enabling you to make sense of situations and to create harmony.

In the Stillness enables you to access and unravel the vast potential of the subconscious and map pathways to the unlimited energy of the Supreme Soul. Through this link with the Supreme Soul, a vast spiritual energy is channelled into your armoury of awareness and spirituality.

In the Stillness inspires and empowers. Use these meditations each day to refresh and regenerate your mind after time in the wider world. They can be used also as a vehicle to send good wishes and powerful thoughts to those in the world who need love, hope and peace.

Jim Ryan
March 2002

In the centre of a dark room,
in front of you,
a candle;
unlit,
encircled by darkness.
Lighting the candle,
a flicker,
a faint glow spreads and warms you.
It is the light of hope.

01 THE CANDLE
You are held,
and slowly drawn to its centre,
and all becomes still.

Gradually the flame increases
and light begins to surround you.
It is the light of love
whose illumination moves deep within you
bringing joy and healing.
The candle flame,
now growing,
begins to fill the room.
It is the light of peace
and all around is quiet
and all around is calm.
And the candlelight again increases
and grows and moves beyond the room
spreading light and love and peace
to those who are caught in the darkness of their

sorrows and fears,
for it is the light of mercy,
the light of compassion,
ever expanding,
evolving
bringing healing and harmony
to the surrounding Earth.

I see around me
a world of tears
and pain
and great sadness
where brothers fight,
and inflict injustice.

The family of mankind
now lies wounded,
on the field of sorrow
and Mother Earth
bends her head in grief.

02 PEACE AND RECONCILIATION

Yet now from its
centre of love —
the centre of light —
the soul opens
its heart centre
and emerges
compassion and mercy
and the purest feelings of goodwill.

Centred in that globe,
in that arc of purest consciousness,
I send pure thoughts

of pure vibration,
of purest love,
that touch all hearts
all minds,
for this is the energy —
the power of true feelings.

It is the light of healing.
It is the light of peace
and hope
and reconciliation,
enabling all to forgive
and to forget
and to resolve all that has occurred
and the light
that is sent —
it fills the darkness.

In that light,
all can see,
and all can feel
the reality,
the way
of true being,
of true brotherhood.

I see the world.
I see my family, my relatives.
I see my friends, workmates and neighbours.
I see all.
I see them with love.

I feel great love flowing from my heart
as I see them,
for I see my brothers and sisters.
I see them with love.

03 VISION OF LOVE

I do not see them with any gross attitude
or with any form of desire or selfishness.
I see them with love.

I see their qualities and their virtues.
I see their kindness and pure feelings.
I see them with love.

I see each one as a unique individual
whose part and role is special to them.
I see them as powerful, spiritual beings.
I see them with love.

I see each one as the beloved child of God
bathed and surrounded
by an almighty and total love.
I see them with that love.

I see them as my brothers.
I see them as my friends.
I see them as my teachers.
I see them as fellow travellers on the spiritual path.
I see them with love.

I help others
with my attitude and thoughts
of good wishes and pure feelings.

04 HELPING

I help others
by abandoning my critical mind
and judgmental vision.

I help others
by allowing my heart
to beat with their heart;
to walk in their shoes;
to see with their eyes.

I help others
by dancing
the dance of harmony;
moving as they move
and appreciating their role;
their effort,
their speciality.

I help others when I play my part
and not another's;
in this
I am left to focus
on what I need to know
and what I need to do
and I realise
that through vibrations
of love, brotherhood and
unlimited compassion
I help myself
by helping others.

15

In all things there is the good.
In each, the jewel of the good
awaits to emerge.
In every action and
in every circumstance
there is the good.
I see it and understand
with the eye of peace and patience
for in all things
there is the good.
Let me stand back,
think less and be still
so my vision fills
with understanding and
my heart fills with mercy.
For in all things there is the good.

For too often the veil of illusion
of outer form
clouds the good.

05 GOODNESS

Let me stand back
think less and be still.
I change the pattern of my response.
I see the benefit, the beauty,
the way for me ahead.
For in all things
there is the good.

I am beautiful and loveable.
I am kind and loving and have a great deal
to share with others.

06 SELF RESPECT

I am talented,
intelligent and creative.
I have many virtues and many qualities.
In the stillness, I reflect on my gifts.
I have the ability to cope with and understand
whatever comes in front of me.
Now I accept myself as I am.
I don't have to please anyone else.
I like myself.
That's what counts.
I am a powerful, loving and creative person.
I am peaceful and light.
I love the world and the world loves me.

I find myself by the seashore.
I am far from the noise and activity of people.
All around is the beauty and harmony of nature.
I have left behind worry and confusion.

07 HEALING POOL

I feel free and light
and at ease with myself and
with everything around me.

Everything seems good — is good.
The sky above is clear and blue.
I walk along the soft, golden sands —
warm and gentle beneath my feet.
All around there is a great feeling of peace
as the waves silently caress the receding sands.
I take in the beauty of that scene
and feel a sense of oneness,
a feeling of love.
Slowly I walk along the sands,
feeling light and good and peaceful.
As the waves wash the sloping land,
I come upon a large cave;
cool fragrances from its centre draw me.
As I look inside, I see a stairway spiralling down.
Sweet scents and gentle colours pull me
as I descend the stairway.
The colours begin to change,
from blue to green to yellow to gold.

I feel light and peaceful.
I arrive at a large opening
and there in front of me is a beautiful pool
of blue water.
This is the pool of eternal healing.
This is the pool of peace.
I am drawn by pure energies
and I gently slide into its still waters.
I float in that stillness — that peace.
The waters of peace flow around me
and over me.
It is the pool of love;
love flows around me and over me.
It is the pool of light.
It is the pool of understanding.
It is the pool of healing.
I glide into the waters.
I sink deep
and am surrounded by pure and powerful vibrations.
I feel light.
Heaviness of the past drops away
as the experience of peace and light
and love begins to fill me,
refresh me and
heal me.
I stay as long as I wish in these healing waters.

Forgetting myself,
I am caught in the lines of others.
I walk in their steps;
think their thoughts;
spin in their turmoil.
I am isolated and
lonely,

08 THE ROLE
stranded between two
vanishing shores.

I need to argue —
to shout at myself.
Let go.
Let go
of the dead.
Let go
and become what I know I am.
I am a soul.

I turn my thoughts away
from the cares and actions of the day,
As I enter into the realm of silence,
I become focused on my inner qualities
— light and love and peace.
My mind becomes still, calm and free
and in this calmness and light
I now can turn my attention higher and beyond.
Letting go of my body and the things of the world,

09 FREE FROM INFLUENCE

I travel to a state
beyond the cosmos,
to a region of purest
light and complete silence.
Here I contact the purest energy,
the light of the supreme consciousness,
the Supreme Soul.
As I make contact with this light,
my thoughts and feelings are held
by the pure love-light energy of that form.
I am absorbed by that radiance,
that power,
that purest energy which surrounds me
and comforts me.
In that orb of purest form
there is only light
and here I am centred and filled
full of light.

There is nothing but light.
I stay in this state for as long as I wish.
In this light I feel myself being healed,
recharged,
rejuvenated
and cleansed.
The sorrows and influences of the past
and old habits diminish and fall away.
I experience being
fulfilled,
satisfied,
with feelings of purest love and highest goodness.
I return to activity,
free of the past,
full of light and love and peace.

I let go of the old images,
the tired, useless words of weakness.
I let go of my pretensions, my fears and my desires
and I stand free. Shorn of artificiality.
I take in and understand the knowledge, the reality,
and the experience of my spiritual form.
I take in and understand the knowledge, the reality,
and the experience of the form
and nature of the Supreme.
I now slip from my chains.
I let go,
for I am free —

10 TRANSFORMATION

free to change,
to move,
to become true.

For now, knowledge,
the sacred drink,
the magic talisman,
the golden apple of legends' immortality,
begins to fill my mind,
encountering,
emerging,
old memory.
As each jewel of sacred wisdom
makes contact,
unfolds,
explodes,

within the inner mind,
a light is lit,
a light begins to grow,
flooding the caverns of my soul.
Soon everywhere there is light,
and light
and light
and the tyrants of the past
that ruled my heart
are now dethroned —
sent into the exile of dark oblivion.
On the throne of my eternal soul
now sits truth's almighty monarch,
bestowing gifts of
peace and love and light,
and the soul in humble homage,
accepts,
and adorns itself
and wears the mantle of the king,
the ruler, now by natural right.
From my heart
there streams
waves of purest feeling —
reaching to the world —
full of compassion, love and light.

11 THE MOUNTAIN AND THE LAKE

The mountain,
resolute,
unshakeable against the fleeing elements,
and below, the lake — earth's mirror —
cool, quiet and
adjusting to each soft wind.
And the two,
like hopeless lovers,
together,
yet, eternally apart,
sharing the beauty of flower and fruit
and scented air.
Yet, now I learn
to integrate,
and drawing that strength and deep tranquillity,
I move towards that highest inspiration;
to skim the clouds
of purest thought
and then to dive and
break the surface of the mind
and become lost in the silence
of the still and peaceful mind.

Thinking of myself
as the form of light
I can move my thoughts
away from my pain
away from the pull of the body.
I let go of my fears.
I let go of the turbulence of my troubled mind
and I move into light
and here there is release
and peace and softness.

12 HEALING

I am free, at ease and tranquil
for here in this place,
in this space of light and love
I am immersed
in the healing energies
of the soul's true state.

I allow the power of love
to emerge, flow and
healing me, recharging me
renewing and re-energising my being.

I allow the power of peace
to emerge and flow
healing me, recharging me
renewing and re-energising my being.

I allow the power of purity
to emerge and flow
healing me, recharging me
renewing and re-energising my being.

In this orb of purest light
I am healed and freed from scars and wounds.
I know that I am not the pain and
the discomfort
that is all with my body.

I let go and move into a condition
where I am not caught
or pulled into despair and self-pity.
But I can now move forward
detached and full of love.

In this state of awareness I know what I need to do.
I feel at peace, completely stable and in control.
I enjoy this sanctuary —
an inner temple of inner healing —
where no pain can come,
no influence,
no darkness,
for in this place within my soul
there is only light and gentle healing
and the purest feelings
of love and peace.

I like myself best
when I'm honest
and true to my own feelings;
when I stand up
and say, with love,
what I think.

I like myself best

13 BEING REAL

when I confront an issue,
yet, don't take issue;
when I support others
who have stood their ground
to share their thoughts.

I like myself best
when I appreciate
another's point of few,
even though we may disagree.

I like myself best
when I let go
of my pretensions
and my false and artificial forms
that smile and nod,
yet, mean the opposite.

I like myself best
when I see a difference,
yet, hold no criticism and
make no personal comment.

I like myself best
when I see others' qualities —
when I see their virtue and their zeal.

I like myself best
when I don't interfere
with another's role —
when I see
and understand and empathise
and realise that they, like me,
need space and
need room to grow —
need others to appreciate their effort.

I like myself best
when I'm not swayed by public opinion —
when I hold my position, my belief —
when I'm not afraid to share it
and then to let it go.

I like myself best
when I think on what's true and real
and hold that close to my heart
and use that in my life.

I guide my thoughts away from the cares of the day,
away from work, plans and projections.
Thoughts of family, friends and connections —
I let them go.
Worries, concerns and fear,
together with the things I think I need,
I move away from their effect and influence.
Now I go inside into the inner room of my mind
where I can be with myself.
In this place I am free and light and peaceful.
Here I have no pressures
no worries

no fears.

14 STRESS FREE

They cannot come here.
In this place of peace,
my thoughts are calm and still and light
and no longer racing and full of imagination.
Here I can think clearly and
see things as they really are.
Here, detached and free
I know what I need to do,
what to think and say.
How and when to act.
With my mind free,
I can now choose my responses carefully.
For here I am peaceful, calm and light.

A thought,
touches
and ripples
the surface of the mind.

15 LAKE OF THE MIND

Yet, in the depths,
far below,
there is a stillness
where no image comes
to echo sadness from the past,
and where no thought desires
to emerge old trauma.
For here the mind
anchored to its original form
is linked in peace.
In this eternal,
timeless space,
old thoughts and forms
and the strutting of the world
fall away
and the soul,
free,
alone,
bathed in the beauty of natural being,
shines
and reflects
the purity
of its angelic light.

Through understanding and experience,
aware of who I am,
of the Great Father,
the source of all virtue and power,
I realise I have all I need.

16 ANGEL LIGHT

In this state of spiritual fullness,
I can share.
I can give what others need.
When I am in light, I can share my light.
When I am in peace, I can share my peace.
Through my mind,
I can radiate waves of love and pure feeling.
Through my face, I can uplift and inspire,
shining with happiness and mercy.
Through words,
I can share jewels of knowledge and inner wisdom,
freeing others from the gaols of confusion.
Filled with spiritual light of the Father,
in the body of light,
I can send light waves, love light,
to the tear-stained lands,
to the sad grey souls,
to light their path,
to warm their hearts,
for this is the light of truth.
It is the light of God.
Now full of light, I share this light, as the Angel of Light.

Now is the dreamtime.
All that has passed
and all that is to come
is part of this dream.
We are all characters,
dreaming in the dream

17 THE DREAMTIME

and every thought
and every action
is a response,

a desire to return,
to go forward,
to recapture
this dream.

Now is the dreamtime.
A time to dream,
to experience,
to find,
the long lost time of being,
when all moved in harmony and natural form.
And now, I journey into silence
to the subtle lands where dreams and truth
are echoes,
shadows,
dissolving,
forming,
becoming what they are.

I see clearly,
the reality, the way, lit,
illuminated,
by the great light,
the one light,
and so I travel
along that way
towards that light
and reaching,
I allow that light
to become my light,
giving me the strength
to fulfil the dream and
to become the dream.

In my form of light, I am light.
In my form of peace, I am peace.
Free of old thoughts
and old memory,
I am free of name, and form, and role.

18 LIGHT ANGEL

I am light.
I am free.
I am detached.
I have no worry, no fear
and no burden.
And so I can ascend
the light beam of pure thought
to the world of pure light.
I have relinquished the world of illusion.
I have let go the old ghosts of the past.
I am free.
Absorbed in silence, I move close
to the light form —
the light centre —
of God's pure form
and draw from the well of unlimited power
and fill, and change, and become;
become what I should be;
become what I want to be;
become what I am —
an angel of light.

I sit with the Seed
in silence, hidden from other eyes.
I grow
nurtured by power and strength and,
from the Seed
the Tree emerges
full of youth and beauty.
The world is one;
a world of lightness and great happiness.
I become part of that world,
a being of subtlety and grace —
serene and content.

19 TREE OF LIFE

The tree expands
into branches,
moving away from unity, from oneness,
and those branches beckon the great masters,
Christ, Buddha, Abraham, Mohammed,
who bring new insight, guidance,
and fresh strength to the Tree.
I learn from them
and draw from their wisdom
the experience of pure love,
the acceptance of the right way of things.
The understanding of the spiritual laws
and the knowledge of the one true Father.
And the Tree grows further
and develops more aspects, more branches,

and the power and the support of former times
begins to change
as spiritual emptiness and sorrow
spreads and affects the Tree.
I feel that.
But I remember my time with the Seed in silence
and these feelings and thoughts
move me and
draw me into a subtle state
away from the darkness and
away from the Tree
and I begin to feel light.
In this state
it is easy to recall,
to return,
to my seed soul state,
to return to the haven of silence,
to the realm of peace.
Here I can link myself
with the great Seed,
the Father of the Tree,
who shelters, protects, empowers me
and through me, begins once again
to restore,
to renew,
to regenerate
the Eternal Tree —
the Tree of Life.

In the form of the true self,
high above,
I drift cloud-like with the soft airs
far beyond the outreach of the dark, dry lands
of the sword-tipped misty mountains.

20 OCEAN RHYTHM

In this light state,
I feel an influence, music,
drawing me to itself;

a gentle,
powerful,
compelling vibration of overwhelming love.
It is the music of the deep.
It is the love call of the Ocean;
calling its cloud children,
come, come,
come my children fill yourself,
come and take from the eternal source.
I, the Keeper of the clouds,
give my children your natural birthright.
So come and fill yourself
from these unfathomable depths
with jewels of purest truth.
Come and take and be fulfilled,
be content and be with me.
Draw up my vibration
and spiritual power;
fill your form,

your being,
with sweetness.
As this call of purest love
resonates deep inside,
the soul becomes a chamber of celestial sound
reverberating to the divine chords
of the Spiritual Father.
Through this union,
my cloud form,
light form,
love form,
soul is filled.
I now glide over the parched, dead lands
of the tired-eyed kings
and shower the gentle waters
of the Spiritual Father,
to bring hope,
freshness and new life.

I am light.
I am a being of light.
My nature is of light.
My home is of light.
I live in light
and in this light
I see the Father who is the Light.

Full of light,

21 LIGHT

reflecting light,
the Bestower of light.
I am drawn to this light.
I experience this light.
I become filled,
recharged,
and power and might
flood my being.
Nothing of darkness is left.
I am filled,
content,
full of light.
There is nothing but light.
I and the Father are one.
I have merged,
become light and am
spreading light all around.

Grey plumes of rising smoke fill a blue sky.
Yellow daffodils nod gently in the pulling breeze,
I am at peace.

22 SUPREME LOVE

Opening my awareness
to the vast world of
consciousness,
to the world of silence,
I feel myself being drawn
onto the great plain of peace,
into the great sea of silence.
My thoughts,
my feelings,
emotions
are calmed and soothed
by gentle waves of purest energy.
The racing heart,
the angry mind,
are eased and cooled,
as the soul floats free
from the demands of the body,
from the effects of the atmosphere,
from the pull of the planet.
There is only peace —
a great peace
filling,
surrounding, merging with the soul.
Stabilised in that peace,

absorbed in that peace,
the soul can now focus
and come close,
to the pure nature,
to the unlimited consciousness,
of the Supreme.
The soul is drawn,
pulled into the upcurrent
of the rays of pure thought,
of pure feeling,
of pure love,
and the soul becomes centred,
surrounded,
and goes deep into that love,
experiences that love,
becomes filled with that love,
becomes that love.
There is nothing but love —
nothing but bliss and light and love.

As I walked the ways of the old world,
life was one of pain and anguish.
Trusting others and the world,
my heart was used,
and hurt,
and torn apart.
Yet God the healer of my heart,
you touch my life,
with the balm of peace,
and purest love.

You soothe,
restore
and heal

23 THE HEALER OF MY HEART

my fractured heart.
For I have travelled long,
and now I'm tired
and have no strength,
no will,
drained,
emptied of all hope,
Yet, God the healer of my heart,
in your lap, you wipe away my tears
and give me rest,
you uplift and fill me
with your love and purest feeling.
You take me into your ocean form,
where I'm lost in the waves

of peace and love and light.
Your soothing waters wash me,
renew me,
recharge me,
and I begin to move,
and think
and smile
and fly.

Eternally still,
dancing on the wave of consciousness,
sought after,
called after,
imprisoned in form,
whose heart beats for all.

Eternally glorious,
centred in silence,

praised by all,

24 HEARTBEAT

blamed by all,
petitioned and ransomed
and treated with scorn,
whose heart beats for all.

Impersonated,
used to justify injustice,
elevated,
adored,
sworn at,
shouted at,
denied and accepted
whose heart beats for all.

Self existent,
benevolent,
beautiful,
yet, cut up,

shared out,
equated with fools,
whose heart beats for all.

Empty and full,
all knowing and innocent,
incredible,
unknowable,
the open door.
No thought,
yet knowing all thought,
whose heart beats for all.

Light form.
Love form.
The mirror,
the master,
the moth,
the death of all deaths,
whose heart beats for all.

Silent,
content,
whose secret fingers,
touch our secret centres,
awakening,
removing,
destroying our sleep,

whispering and singing,
entreating us to dance,
whose heart beats for all.

Beyond limit and weakness,
the cosmic mover,
the loving child,
whose heart beats for all.

Touching,
yet, untouched,
giving,
but not receiving,
taking,
but not accumulating,
acting,
but beyond all action,
the ocean,
the seed,
whose heart beats for all.

In stillness,
unchanging,
watching the illusion,
watching the game,
whose heart beats for all.

Moving through time,
in differing forms and roles,
in relationships of ease,
and loveful harmony,
I see myself,
the soul,
on life's great stage,
among changing scenes
unchanging.

25 DIVINE VISION

I observe the play
of soul and matter,
linked and fused,
by actions law,
each part and form,
unique and lovely
flowing and responding,
to the eternal rhythms of eternal time.
And I stand detached,
and watch,
and I'm at peace.
For I see the past,
and the present,
and I see the future,
and all is good,
and all is well.
I see
and I'm at peace.

From this unlimited state,
I understand,
and see all forms
all linked into life's eternal stream,
and beyond all
I now can see the absolute form,
of the absolute Father,
I see this light and love and power,
and I begin to understand,
to recognise,
His role,
His way,
and I start to see how all can change,
how all can emerge their purest form by
drawing from supreme love
and I realise
that I too can change my thoughts,
my words,
my life,
and that new experience
becomes my world;
and so the world changes.

The great sun in its misty frame
warms the ancient rocks,
gently stroking the hanging leaves
and high in the heavens
a songbird soars

26 FLYING BIRD

gliding into the distant blue.
My vision too is caught
and travels.

I leave thoughts of self and the old lands
and fly beyond
into the realm of light,
the realm of silence
where the great sun,
the Great Father,
draws me into His orbit of unlimited light
into the centre of His unlimited Heart
and that light and that love
enables me to fly eternally, constantly
above the turmoil and confusions
of the lower worlds.
I am the flying bird.

In the innermost cave
of the inner self,
in that subtlest state of light,

27 SECRET CHAMBER

there is no desire,
no feeling
to accumulate,
to possess,
and become part of the merry-go-round
of loss and gain and
of name and fame,
where life is empty,
devoid of spiritual strength,
constantly seeking, searching,
fanning the flames,
of insatiable greed.
Now all this I leave,
and journey inwards,
towards the secret chamber of the soul,
to discover, to reclaim,
the long lost treasures of eternal truth.
The jewels,
the pearls of purest peace,
the golden crown of eternal light,
and most of all,
the master ring,
the ruling ring,
of God's own love.

From the heights,
the chattering rooks
drop into the stillness
of the valley deep,
cut by the slow,
meandering rivers,

passage to the sea,

28 HARMONY

and I too,
let my thoughts go,

to become free,
to move
into space,
into light,
and then to fall,
to drop deep
into the abyss of silence,
linking into
the stream of purest consciousness,
dissolving,
reassembling,
returning to the essence,
the oneness of true being.
In my heart there resonates a deep love
emerging a wonderful feeling
of harmony,
a coming together
with all things.

I open my mind to eternal truth
and its fragrance revives and uplifts my heart.
As I flow and ascend on the up-current
                of unfolding wisdom

29 TRUTH

feelings of hope and joy
                and freedom emerge.
I focus my thoughts and feelings
on the truth,
on the nature
of my eternal being
and I feel lightness and stability
and a great sense of serenity, peace and easiness
settling on my mind.
I focus my thoughts and feelings
on the truth,
on the nature
of the unlimited form
and being of God
and I feel empowered, protected,
full of light.
I focus my thoughts and feelings
on the eternal truth of the law of karma,
cause and effect.
I understand and am full with satisfaction
knowing that, from whatever is done
and whatever is experienced
each receives their return.

All is just and all is right
and now I know what I need to do.
I focus my thoughts and feelings
on the power of thought
and I realise and understand
that my life is the product of my thoughts.
Now that my thoughts are full of the waves of truth
I now can create and
I can experience
a life full of power, of peace and of love.
I send these energies, these waves of power
to the world and I feel full of bliss,
full of joy —
content and happy.

The stillness of all things
pulls me into silence.

30 PERFECTION

I glide into that space
and become part of the
stillness
where everything is held as
part of a perfect
mosaic of natural order.
I hold that moment.
I feel part of everything
and everything feels a part of me.
I expand into all
and I reduce the all
into the essence of my being.
And all things are as they are.

Turning the mind away from the turbulence
of change,
I open the door of awareness
and begin my journey into light.
And in this light I begin to see
and in this light I begin to know
that I am the form of light.
Thinking on this light
I increase my light.

31 WISDOM

It is the light of love.
It is the light of peace.
That love and that peace and that
light fill me completely
and take me beyond.
This awakened light, my light,
pulls me, draws me to the source of light,
to the light of the Supreme,
whose light is the light of knowledge
and total wisdom.
Connected and centred, that Supreme light
invades my light.
It fills my mind.
It uplifts my heart.
In this lotus light,
in this lotus heart,
seated on the throne of peace

I begin to understand
to know the meaning and significance of all things,
I see the play,
the acts and the actors,
the great movement of cause and effect,
the spinning of the cycle of eternal time.
I see myself
and the Father — my friend.
I now no longer desire to search, to question
for I now feel content,
peaceful and at one with all.

From the faraway land,
I travel
to this drama stage.
I am the observer.
I watch and see
the actors and the actions,
the comings and goings;
who moves and uses,
and shares and takes.

32 DETACHED AND LOVING

I am
detached,
the observer.

My subtle, soul light form,
sees, holds
but does not need;
is not dependent
on the forms,
the structures,
the circumstances,
of the material plane.
I see the expectations,
the confusions,
the colliding parts
yet I stand back,
detached,
knowing that each one is the shaper,
the creator,

the reconciler of their part.
I stand back,
hold back,
full of love.
I cannot play their part
or change the scenes.
But in my state of self awareness,
linked to the restorative centre,
of God's pure light,
I can give support and strength
and send that light,
from the realm of light,
to guide,
to inspire,
to help move the illusion,
so that all can dance,
and all can sing,
and fly to the world of light.

A figure moves.
The wind blows.
I watch and see
the rhythms and flows
of natural order.
I watch and see.

A child cries.

33 OBSERVER

Upheaval
and a sudden shift
to darkness,
I watch and see
with no reaction,
no impulse to interfere
for new forms come,
new patterns,
structures,
fresh flows,
and all things change.
So I watch and see
with patience and with love.

I hear my thoughts.
I speak my mind.
I take a stance.
This is my world.
Yet subtle voices,
thoughts,
ideas of other philosophy,
come floating on the current
turning
emerging,
revealing
new aspects,
ideas not formerly held.

34 COUNTERPOINT

I let go,
move forward,
explore

and find
those ripples,
those swirling eddies of new awareness,
making contact,
making sense;
there is a fusion
of two worlds
merging,
becoming one,
yet, separate.

Both intrinsic to the other,
reflections of the other;
Truth's eternal twin.
And now,
I live,
I move
between two points,
experiencing one truth,
holding,
in harmony,
in oneness,
the jewelled perspective
of the single pure moment.

A shift.
A movement,
imperceptible,
a subtle flick of the turning mind,

35 STILLNESS

thoughts spreading out
on a vast plain,
expanding,
breaking apart,
having no connection,
losing momentum,
unable to run —
and as each thought form
begins to melt,
lose shape,
and become absorbed
by the plain of stillness,
into the softness of silence,
there is Peace.

In the room of my mind
I enclose my thoughts, resting
in stillness.

The functioning body begins to ease.

36 SILENCE

My breathing becomes slower,
my senses relax,
and the inner body feels cool and peaceful.
As thoughts lie slumbering
in their bed of peace
no words come tumbling.
The mind is still
and energy is preserved.
In this centre, I feel fullness,
a binding
a realignment, of the soul's discordant parts.
Within the inner recesses of the inner soul,
a power grows,
an energy,
of purest consciousness,
which flows,
like a silver stream of silent sound,
echoing,
sounding,
filling,
taking the soul,
into the silence of being complete.

I walk the path of peace.
The way ahead is clear.
The autumn woods
evoke old memory;
feelings of warmth and oneness,
of times long gone,
draw me to a subtler state.

I reflect

37 RENEWAL   and see

how nature changes,

moves,
unquestioning.
Evolving,
developing,
becoming,
and then — letting go
of beauty's form,
moves into silence,
returning to the seed,
to the form
of its renewal.

And in that silence,
in that state of purest being,
waits
protected,
held
by the power of natural order,
waiting
to be released
to emerge,
to come again.
And so now
I walk that way —
the way of silence.

JIM RYAN has more than 20 years international experience working with corporations, local authorities and government organisations as a Human Resources trainer and an Educationalist.

ABOUT THE AUTHOR

He has worked in a diverse range of educational establishments to the level of Principal. Since the early 1980s, he has been a student and teacher of meditation and metaphysics and conducted seminars and workshops in many countries. His presentations combine humour, philosophy and practical strategies. His love for literature and poetry shines in the light of his Irish eyes!

PHOTOGRAPHY THANKS TO
Peter Damo pages 27, 45 and 63
Michael Murphy pages 15, 21, 33, 39, 51 and 57
Kathy Willoughby pages 9 and 69
and to Bruce and Suzanne Willoughby
for their loungeroom

Other Eternity Ink meditation books, tapes and CDs are available.
For a catalogue contact:
Eternity Ink, 77 Allen Street, Leichhardt NSW Australia 2040
Email: bkmedia@ozemail.com.au
www.brahmakumaris.com.au or www.bkwsu.com

Eternity Ink is the publisher for the Brahma Kumaris World Spiritual University.
If you wish to find out about the free meditation courses offered by the
Brahma Kumaris World Spiritual University, contact the main centre closest to you:

UK:	International Co-ordinating Office, 65 Pound Lane, London, NW10 2HH, UK Tel (20) 8727 3350 Email: london@bkwsu.com
AUSTRALIA:	78 Alt Street, Ashfield, Sydney NSW 2131 Tel (2) 9716 7066 Email: indra@brahmakumaris.com.au
BRAZIL:	R. Dona Germaine Burchard, 589 – Sao Paulo, SP 05002-062, Tel (11) 3864 3694 Email: saopaulo@bkumaris.com.br
CHINA:	17 Dragon Road, Causeway Bay, Hong Kong Tel (852) 2806 3008 Email: rajainfo@rajayoga.com.hk
INDIA:	25 New Rohtak Road, Karol Bagh, New Delhi, 1100055 Tel (11) 355 0355 Email: bkpbd@vsnl.com
KENYA:	Global Museum, Maua Close, off Parklands Road, Westlands, Nairobi Tel (2) 743 572 Email: bkwsugm@holidaybazaar.com
RUSSIA:	2 Gospitalnaya Ploschad, Building 1, Moscow 111020 Tel (95) 263 02 47 Email: bkwsu@mail.ru
USA:	Global Harmony House, 46 Sth Middle Neck Rd, Great Neck NY 11021 Tel (516) 773 0971 Email: newyork@bkwsu.com